£G99

HUNTING
TEXTILE
DESIGNS

the

BY ANTHONY CHAN
WITH AN INTRODUCTION BY
NORMA LIVO

Stemmer
House
Publishers

Gilsum, NH 03448

INTRODUCTION

The Hmong people have always been a minority wherever they lived. Many individuals of this indigenous people, with their own unique culture, history and art, are being rapidly absorbed into the American culture as part of their new life in the United States.

The hallmark of Hmong history in crafts is the pa ndau or flower cloth. For centuries, it has been the tradition of these hilltribes to give a square of elaborate handstitching to a neighbor as a gift, to celebrate a significant event such as a birth or marriage.

The pa ndau is a complex form of textile art. It incorporates applique, reverse applique, cross-stitching, batik and embroidery. Three or four layers of cloth may be used. Designs include geometric patterns and symbolic representations, as well as those generally based on the natural environment.

In this overview of the Hmong and their vanishing way of life, we will look at some of the history, beliefs, culture and folk art of this proud people.

Hmong History

The Hmong (pronounced *mung*) of Southeast Asia are some of the most recent United States immigrants. Originally they migrated to Southeast Asia from their ancient homeland in China. Some of their songs suggest that the Hmong's origins were possibly in Mongolia.

This independent people settled in the mountainous terrain of Burma, Laos, Thailand and Vietnam. Some say the name Hmong means "free man." In all their travels they never integrated with the societies around them, choosing to remain free and independent. However, their culture was enriched by adaptations of local traditions.

The Hmong have a long and distinguished history as lovers of freedom; recently, as fighters for the United States and its allies during the Vietnam war. The Hmong disdained being soldiers and served as labor forces to repair roads during the French colonial period. Whenever the government sent requisitions for young men to fill military or work forces, the Hmong would try to hire replacements. It wasn't until the Laotian civil war in 1959 that the Hmong became affected by national politics.

The United States recruited and trained the Hmong into a tough fighting and intelligence gathering force. Operating against the Communists, the Hmong were known as the CIA's "secret army."

In this role, the Hmong sabotaged war supplies moving along the Ho Chi Minh Trail and rescued American pilots downed over Laos. As United States allies, the Hmong stood firm in the fiercest fighting and suffered enormous casualties. During the late 1960s, the war in Laos intensified and the Hmong were doing the bulk of American fighting. Estimates note that the Hmong suffered a ten times higher casualty rate than United States forces.

When the Americans pulled out of Indochina, the Hmong found themselves the target of genocide by the Communist troops because of their stance as United States allies. Beginning in 1976, many Hmong escaped to Thailand by crossing the Mekong River. In 1980 alone, at the height of the refugee crisis, more than 20,000 Hmong came to the United States.

The Hmong are now settled in such cities as Denver, Minneapolis, Washington, D.C. and Fresno. Since the young Hmong have been forced to concentrate their time and energies adapting to Western culture, seeking education and employment, they generally are not learning and practicing their folk arts.

Until the late 1950s, the Hmong had their own Hmong oral language but no written language. Consequently they have used stories, songs and their arts traditionally to pass on their history.

Hmong Beliefs

The Hmong are animistic. They live in a world populated with spirits. There are two words for spirit. The first word is "da," which is used for dead or passed-away spirits in need of religious rituals to free them from the earth.

The other spirit term, "plih," is used for the spirit of someone living. However, it can also be used for non-persons' spirits, such as crops, wealth and animals. When used for these objects, "plih" translates to "force."

There are spirits everywhere. Along a trail, a bad spirit can cause you to sprain your ankle. If a hunter shoots an animal, he smears blood on his crossbow to placate and show respect for the animal's spirit.

There are also spirit trees. The Hmong string white cloth and strings all over them to identify them. In the United States a new Hmong family saw a tree covered with toilet paper and were joyous because they thought it was a spirit tree.

Spirits dwell in the Hmong homes as well. Every house is inhabited by two spirits they respect. There is the spirit of the front door and the spirit of the house altar "suka." This altar has to be on the side of the wall opposite the front door. Water, drink, incense and offerings are placed on the suka.

Spirits affect Hmong conduct in many ways. Moments after birth, every baby receives a simple necklace. The necklace locks the spirit and life into the body.

The Hmong have a custom of tying strings around each other's wrists at special events. This symbolically confines their protective spirits inside their bodies. This practice, called "baci," is similar to the thong-tying practice used by the Iroquois tribe before their storytelling sessions. The Iroquois also used the thong-tying ritual to keep the spirit in the body during the storytelling. The Hmong baci tradition was adapted from the Laotians.

Hmong Textile Arts

The Hmong traditional ethnic clothing has tremendous cultural history. The Hmong are bearers of a living culture that carries centuries of information. This storehouse is continually growing and changing — folklore at work.

The creation of their stitchery and textile art takes time and skill. The Hmong costumes and textiles are a statement about women's time, about the priorities of their culture, and the value they have attached to the art form. Above all, the cultural values of perseverance and hard work are exemplified in their elaborate stitchery.

Young girls spend many years learning the sewing techniques and traditional designs necessary for the creation of the Hmong costume. The artist uses very thin needles about one inch in length. At courting time, the beauty and intricacy of a girl's needlework invite admiration and assure her of a favored suitor. The greater a girl's needlework skill, the more value she has as a wife.

The finest needlework is devoted to marriage and death. At marriage, the bride's parents must provide her costume. At death the Hmong are buried in full costume to ensure that they will be recognized in the afterlife. Married daughters and the daughters-in-law are held responsible for providing the death costume for parents. This shows proper respect for the dead to the community.

The death costume includes a white robe that covers from head to ankle. There is also a skirt, shirt and a pa ndau used as a pillow cover. Other pa ndau pieces are also placed on top of the body.

Babies are prized possessions and are sometimes compared with flowers. The birth of a new baby is an occasion to create an elaborate baby carrier, to be used to strap the baby close to the mother's back. These carriers are usually rectangualr in shape, approximately 16″ by 23″, with a smaller rectangle stitched across one end. The borders of these carriers are usually of several colors. one stitched to the other and accented with embellishments. Long bright sashes are attached to the carriers and wrapped around the mother's body to hold the baby securely in place. The large rectangle supports the baby's body and the small rectangle supports the child's neck. The parents of the new mother are the givers of this baby carrier.

Another article of apparel, the child's hat, tells much about Hmong tradition and beliefs. The typical hat is a black fabric skull-cap, covered with embellishments of applique, cross-stitches, pom-poms, coins or beads.

According to legend, the child's hat is quite colorful, so that the spirits looking down from above will think that it is a flower. Another legend says that these bright hats encourage the kindly flower spirits to descend and inhabit the baby itself. In any case, the legends have fostered a tradition of Hmong craftsmanship in stitchery.

The New Year's festival is a very special event. The harvest is in and a new year is ahead. It is believed that Hmong who wear old clothing at the festival may have bad luck during the year. Therefore, a new round of sewing is needed to provide the traditional elaborate costumes.

Pa Ndau

As mentioned earlier, the pa ndau or flower cloth is handmade history. This complex form of textile art uses designs based on Hmong beliefs, the world around them, geometric patterns and symbolic representations.

The designs that contain traditional patterns are highly symbolic. For example, the snail design is a symbol of family growth and interrelatedness; the center of the coil symbolizes the ancestors, while the outer spirals are the successive generations. The double snail shell represents the union of two families. It also symbolizes the spinning motion used in many spiritual chants.

The elephant's foot, according to some, is a symbol of family wealth. The rooster is considered a feisty protector. There are many designs from nature as well as geometric designs, such as triangles, which are used to represent teeth, fish scales, a fence or a protective barrier to keep the good spirits in and the evil forces out. There are tracks which are considered the spirit imprint of the person or animal who has passed by. Tiger paw prints are spirit imprints of tigers — the greatest threat to a small village. Centipedes are known for their medicinal qualities and are highly respected. The dream-maze, which repeats a pattern of right-angled appliques (legend has it that a Hmong woman awoke from a dream to cut out a new and different pattern), is used for burial clothing.

A diamond in a square represents the altar maintained in the home (or the floor plan of a Buddhist pagoda, or the spirit imprint of the most powerful of the good spirits); the snail-and-pumpkin-seed pattern is found on children's hats. Their young souls tend to wander and this pattern bonds their souls to their heads until they are used to their environment.

The fish hook symbolizes a young girl's hope of finding a suitor. The eight-pointed star is sometimes referred to as the "left star" and indicates good luck. It is also known as a protective symbol.

The protective armor of the dragon represents the mythical dragon that lives forever, knows nothing of sickness, and is respected by all.

Traditionally, when a hunter goes hunting, he must wear a small piece of pa ndau to keep his spirit from being transformed into an animal. Otherwise, another hunter could kill the transformed animal and end his life.

The Hmong needle artist is similar to the Navajo weaver of tradition. Sometimes the Hmong change color slightly on a corner of the work to let the spirit of the person making it escape. For example, on a tree trunk included in a much larger scene, there is a tiny rectangle of different colored thread. Some say this is no accident but carefully sewn there to follow beliefs.

The large hangings which are covered with pictorial representations appear to be a form which was used only fairly recently. This form is now seen increasingly. Each large size pa ndau may take three to four months to construct, totaling over 500 hours of work for even a skilled worker.

Among the large pa ndau are "storycloths." Some of them, made in the refugee camps of Thailand, tell ancient myths. Others show what life was like in their villages before the war.

They also depict courtship games, weddings, ritual sacrifice, feasting with the baci (tying of strings around the wrists) ceremony and other rituals.

Some of this narrative needlework shows farming scenes, crops grown and harvested. There are also motifs which include people in contact with the CIA, getting guns, participating in battles, and then waving farewell to the CIA people. These scenes are followed by pictures of escape from Laos, crossing the Mekong River to Thailand (in a variety of ways), reaching the resettlement camps, and tearful departure for other countries. Many of these cloths have captions in broken English.

All of these storycloth pa ndau are new expressions of storytelling from a people with a rich oral tradition. The Hmong women make a strong, powerful statement about their lives and struggles in these pieces.

Storycloths began to appear in the United States during the late 1970 s. It is suggested that these new expressions in stitchery are the result of commercial appeal. The stories in stitchery are more marketable than abstract, geometric designs, and these pieces are intended for export sales. More recent subject matter for pa ndau motif is the life of Christ. Large cloths depict the birth of Jesus, and continue to show the story of his life and death. Obviously these are intended to attract Christian buyers.

There are also works with Christmas tree, shamrock, Valentine Day and dinosaur designs. Marketing has also shifted stitchery from articles of clothing made for themselves, to decorative needlework such as wall hangings, bedspreads, pillow covers, eyeglass cases, book marks, tablecloths, belts and appliques for western apparel. The Hmong are adapting and innovating.

In the storycloths, people and animals tend to appear in profile. That is not to say that variations do not appear. Even though there seemingly is a stereotyped approach to the figures and scenes, individual artists' touches are evident.

During the summer of 1988 a large pa ndau purchased at the night market in Chaing Mai, Thailand, from a pa ndau shop, used graceful figures, full-faces, and a much less intense approach to the art. The cloths can exhibit a delightful exuberance and playfulness, demonstrating that the Hmong not only survive but also celebrate life.

Workmanship varies also. The quality test is to draw a thumbnail over a design to see if the stitches are tight. If they are, they will not reveal any of the background material.

Changes in fabrics and colors have taken place in recent times. Home-grown indigo dye decreed that much of the Hmong cloth ranged in color shades from black to light blue. Bright colors became popular once they were available through traders. Many art pieces are being created using the colors of the American flag. Red, white and blue combinations were not used prior to the contact with Americans. The war had its impact on the choice of material also. Some of the tapestries use military sleeping-bag fabric and material from parachutes, as well as rice sack material.

Because of the impact of war, isolation, resettlement and other changes in their lives, what was true last year may well be changed this year. Many of the symbolic meanings have been lost. While one person interprets the design with one meaning, another person will give that same design another interpretation. The Hmong stitchery is a changing record of their history and culture, and it must be appreciated for the social information it provides.

Hmong needlework is also influenced by artistic originality and this allows for continual expansion and new directions for their art. As the Hmong live and work in our country, their traditions are fading. We can only hope that their heritage and culture can be preserved and appreciated through their art and stories. If we recognize what we are seeing, we will understand much more about these special people.

N.J.L.

PLATES

All works are of the twentieth century and are from the Norma J. Livo collection.

Plate 1. Traditional designs. Artist and provenance unknown. 18″ x 18″. Symbolic designs: upper left, snailshells (symbolizes extended family and its growth) and step designs; upper right, centipede (highly respected for medicinal qualities) borders with snailshells; lower left, snailshells and waterlilies; lower right, clams with snailshells.

Plate 2. Traditional designs. Artist and provenance unknown. 18″ x 18″. Symbolic designs: upper left, star with snailshells and heart motif; upper right, snailshells; lower left, fireworks; lower right, snailshells with dog's foot in corners.

Plate 3. Traditional designs. Artist and provenance unknown. 18″ x 18″. Symbolic designs: upper left, cucumber seed; upper right, geometric maze; lower left, dream maze; lower right, centipede border with sample crosses and spinning wheel design.

Plate 4. Traditional designs. Artist and provenance unknown. 18″ x 18″. Symbolic designs: upper left, hearts; upper right, cobweb and hearts; lower left, hearts and dragon's tail ring; lower right, hearts.

Plate 5. Traditional design. Artist and provenance unknown. 18″ x 18″. Symbolic designs: upper left, elephant's footprint (associated with great wealth) with plumes; upper right, elephant's footprints with dog's foot in the corners; lower left, elephant's footprint with diamonds in a square (the diamonds in the square can represent the altar maintained in the home or the imprint of the most powerful good spirit); lower right, elephant's footprint with pinwheels in the corners.

Plate 6. Traditional designs. Artist and provenance unknown. 18″ x 18″. Symbolic designs: upper left, ram's head with snailshells and diamond in a square; upper right, elephant's foot with ram's head with triangle border (this can represent teeth, fish scales, mountains, etc., to symbolize a protective barrier); lower left, ram's heads and snailshells; lower right, entwined ram's head with elephant's foot and heart motif.

Plate 7. Traditional design. Artist, Mayhnia Ly of Denver. 16″ x 16″. Symbolic design: spiderweb with a variety of borders.

Plate 8. Traditional design. Artist and provenance unknown. 4′ x 3′. Old people's design.

Plate 9. Images of a forest with a variety of flora and fauna. Artist unknown. Made in a Thailand resettlement camp. 5′ x 5′. Details of one of the scenes.

Plate 10. Images of a forest with a variety of flora and fauna. Artist unknown. Made in Thailand resettlement camp. 8′ x 8′. Details from one of the scenes.

Plate 11. Agricultural scenes. Artist unknown. Made in a Thailand resettlement camp. 6′ x 6′. Details of some of the plants.

Plate 12. Animals. Artist unknown. Made in a Thailand resettlement camp. 5′ x 4′. Representation of animals including variations from modern times. Creatures such as kangaroos and occasional dinosaurs demonstrate influences from other places. Some of these are copied from pictures and books.

Plate 13. Water dragons. Artist unknown. Ban Vanai resettlement camp in Thailand 8′ x 8′. This is a detail from a story cloth based on a folkstory.

Plate 14. Orphan boy playing the keng. Artist unknown. Ban Vanai resettlement camp in Thailand. 8′ x 8′. This is a detail from the folkstory "Why Farmers Have to Work so Hard."

Plate 15. Birds. Artist unknown. Made in a Thailand resettlement camp. 5′ x 4′. Representation of fantastic birds in a forest.

Plate 16. Bird family. Artist unknown. Made in Ban Vanai resettlement camp in Thailand. 6′ x 6′. This is a detail from the folkstory cloth of "A Bird Couple's Vow."

Plate 17. Animals by a stream coming down from the mountains. Artist unknown. From a resettlement camp in Thailand. 6′ x 5′. This scene is full of creatures with symbolic meaning to the Hmong. For instance, the tortoise is the most truthful messenger, who brings advice from the spirit world and the ancestors.

Plate 18. Composite of details. Artist unknown. From a resettlement camp in Thailand. 8′ x 8′. This scene is full of cultural and creature representations.

Plate 19. Birds. Artist unknown. Made in a Thailand resettlement camp. 5′ x 4′. Representation of fantastic birds in a forest.

Plate 20. Birds. See plate 19.

Plate 21. Nature scenes. Artist unknown. Made in a Thailand resettlement camp. 6′ x 6′. A composite of creatures and plants that are symbolic. For instance, the crab covers the opening to the sky through which the flood waters pass.

Plate 22. Forest scenes. Artist unknown. Made in a Thailand resettlement camp. 8′ x 8′. The whole pa ndau is full of scenes like this and the colors are replete with lime greens, hot pinks and bright yellows.

Plate 23. Cultural information. Artist unknown. Made in Ban Vanai resettlement camp. 8′ x 6′. This pa ndau has a map of Laos in the center and cultural details all around it, designating the regional clothing, agriculture and festivals.

Plate 24. Farming and Gathering. Artist unknown. Thailand resettlement camp. 8′ x 6′. This pa ndau details agricultural scenes, harvesting scenes and wood gathering.

Plate 25. Farming and Gathering. See plate 24.

Plate 26. Farming and Gathering. See plate 24. The humor of the aquaduct from the mountains ending in a pond with ducks ("aquaducks") was a point of humor made by the Hmong seller.

Plate 27. Farming and Gathering. See plate 24.

Plate 28. Farming and Gathering. See plate 24.

Plate 29. Farming and Gathering. See plate 24.

Plate 30. Farming and Gathering. See plate 24.

Plate 31. The War. Artist unknown. Ban Vanai resettlement camp. 6′ x 8′. This pa ndau is divided into scenes of the war. Graphic details include the exploding body on the bottom.

Plate 32. From the same war storycloth. It depicts the U.S. pulling out, the escape across the Mekong River, arrival in Thailand, resettlement camp and then immigration to the United States.

Plate 33. A Bird Couple's Vow. Artist unknown. Ban Vanai resettlement camp. 8′ x 8′. These are scenes from the folkstory cloth of the bird couple's vow and reincarnation.

Plate 34. Folkstory. Artist unknown. Ban Vanai resettlement camp. 8′ x 8′. This is a scene from a folkstory in which the Hmong Orphan Boy captures a bride.

Plate 35. Customs. Artist unknown. Ban Vanai resettlement camp. 8′ x 8′. These are scenes from cultural traditions showing the ball-throwing game played by young people during the New Year's Festival. The bottom scene depicts a newlywed couple leaving for the groom's house. The souls and good fortune of the young couple are enfolded inside the umbrella tied with the black-and-white striped turban band of the bride.

Plate 36. See plate 34. The cultural traditions represented here include the rooster being waved over the bride as she enters the groom's home to finalize her admission as a member of the groom's household. The scene at the table is called *baci;* strings are tied around each other's wrists as a blessing is given. The shaman is performing rites at the altar.

Plate 37. The Flood Story. Artist unknown. Made in a Thailand resettlement camp. 5′ x 6′. The story of the flood and the repopulation of the earth is given on this pa ndau. English was used to go along with the art.

Plate 38. The Bird Couple's Vow. Artist unknown. Ban Vanai resettlement camp. 8′ x 8′. This is the story of the bird couple, their reincarnation and how they lived happily ever after. Again, it is accompanied with English text.

Plate 39. Lazy Joua. Artist unknown. Ban Vanai resettlement camp. 8′ x 7′. This folkstory is also accompanied with English text.

Plate 40. See plate 39.

Plate 41. See plate 33.

Plate 42. Yer and the Tiger. Artist unknown. Ban Vanai resettlement camp. 4′ x 6′. This folkstory has the English text and the colors of the tiger are intense.

Plate 43. See plate 42.

Escape. Artist unknown. Made in a Thailand resettlement camp. 6′ x 5′. This is a scene of the Hmong traveling through the forest as they head for Thailand and escape.

1

3

4

8

11

19

BLUE HMONG XIENG KHOUANG

STIPPED HMONG HUA PHAN

MIEN   HMONG LUANG PRABANG

WHITE HMONG XIENG KHOUANG

LUE

LAO

23

29

34

A LOT OF WATER FELL FROM THE SKY AND COVERED THE WHOLE WORLD. ALL PEOPLE DIED EXCEPT A BROTHER AND A SISTER ESCAPED IN A WOODEN DRUM THAT FLOAT.

THEY CAME OUT AFTER THE RAIN.

THEY WORKED HARD AND STARTED A NEW LIFE TOGETHER.

AFTER MANY YEARS THEY WERE LONELY. THEY WANTED MORE PEOPLE. THE BROTHER SAID "IF YOU MARRY ME WE CAN HAVE MORE PEOPLE."

THE SISTER SAID «WE EACH THROW A STONE DOWN OPPOSITE SIDE OF THE HILL. IF THE STONES COME BACK TOGETHER WE WILL MARRY. BUT I DON'T THINK THIS COULD HAPPEN.»

THE BROTHER PUT THE STONES TOGETHER AT NIGHT. NEXT MORNING THEY SAW THE STONES TOGETHER.

THEY WERE MARRIED AND WERE NOT LONELY BECAUSE THEY HAD MORE PEOPLE AND MORE ANIMALS LIKE THOSE IN HMONG.

ONCE UPON A TIME THERE WAS A FAMILY OF BIRDS IN A FOREST

ONE DAY THE HUSBAND BIRD WENT TO FIND FOOD FOR HIS FAMILY.

SUDDENLY THE FLOWER CLOSED. HE WAS CAUGHT INSIDE.

WHILE HE WAS GONE, A FIRE BURNED THE FOREST. HIS WIFE AND HIS BABY CHICKS DIED.

THE NEXT MORNING, THE FLOWER OPENED. THE HUSBAND BIRD CAME BACK.

HE WAS VERY SAD.

HE SAID---«NEXT LIFE I MUST BE HER HUSBAND AGAIN» THEN HE FLEW TO THE FIRE ALSO.

IN THE SECOND LIFE THE WIFE WAS BORN AS A PRINCESS, BUT SHE DIDN'T SPEAK TO ANY MALE EVEN HER FATHER THE KING. HER NAME WAS YER.

THE HUSBAND WAS BORN AS A POOR MAN. HIS NAME WAS DROW CHOUA.

ONCE THERE WAS A LAZY MAN NAMED JOUA. HE WENT TO THE EDGE OF THE RIVER AND PUT SAND OVER HIMSELF EXCEPT HIS EYES.

A HAWK CAME TO REST AND WAS CAUGHT BY JOUA.

THE HAWK WAS AFRAID AND TOLD JOUA THAT IF HE RELEASED IT, IT WOULD GIVE HIM A MAGICAL STONE.

JOUA RELEASED IT, THE HAWK GAVE HIM A MAGICAL STONE.

JOUA ASKED THE STONE TO GIVE FOOD.

JOUA TOOK THE FOOD HOME AND THEY ENJOYED THE FOOD.

AFTERWARD JOUA WENT TO SLEEP AS USUAL.

A FEW MONTHS LATER, THERE WAS A WAR IN THE KINGDOM, THE KING COULD NOT FIGHT THE AGGRESSION.

THE KING ASED JOUA TO HELP HIM THE SERVANTS CARRIED JOUA TO THE PALACE.

JOUA RECEIVED VICTORY, BECAUSE OF THE MAGIC STONE

NOW THEY LIVED PEACEFULLY

THEY CELEBRATED HIS VICTORY.

THEN THE KING DIVIDED A PART OF HIS KINGDOM TO JOUA. JOUA BECAME A KING.

Colophon
Designed by Barbara Holdridge
Composed in Times Roman by Brown Composition, Inc.,
    Baltimore, Maryland
Color separations by GraphTec, Baltimore, Maryland
Printed on 75-pound Williamsburg Offset and bound by BookCrafters
    Fredericksburg, Virginia